PONY MONEY

(SECOND REVISED EDITION)

FIRST EDITION BY:

BOOKBABY PUBLISHING

7905 NORTH ROUTE 130

PENNSAUKEN, NJ 08110

866.905.2446

FIRST EDITION ISBN #: 978-1-54397-360-0

BOOKBABY PUBLISHING

7905 N CRESCENT BLVD

PENNSAUKEN, NJ 08110

877.961.6878

info@bookbaby.com

ISBN #: PRINT: 978-1-66783-320-0

eISBN #: 978-1-66783-321-7

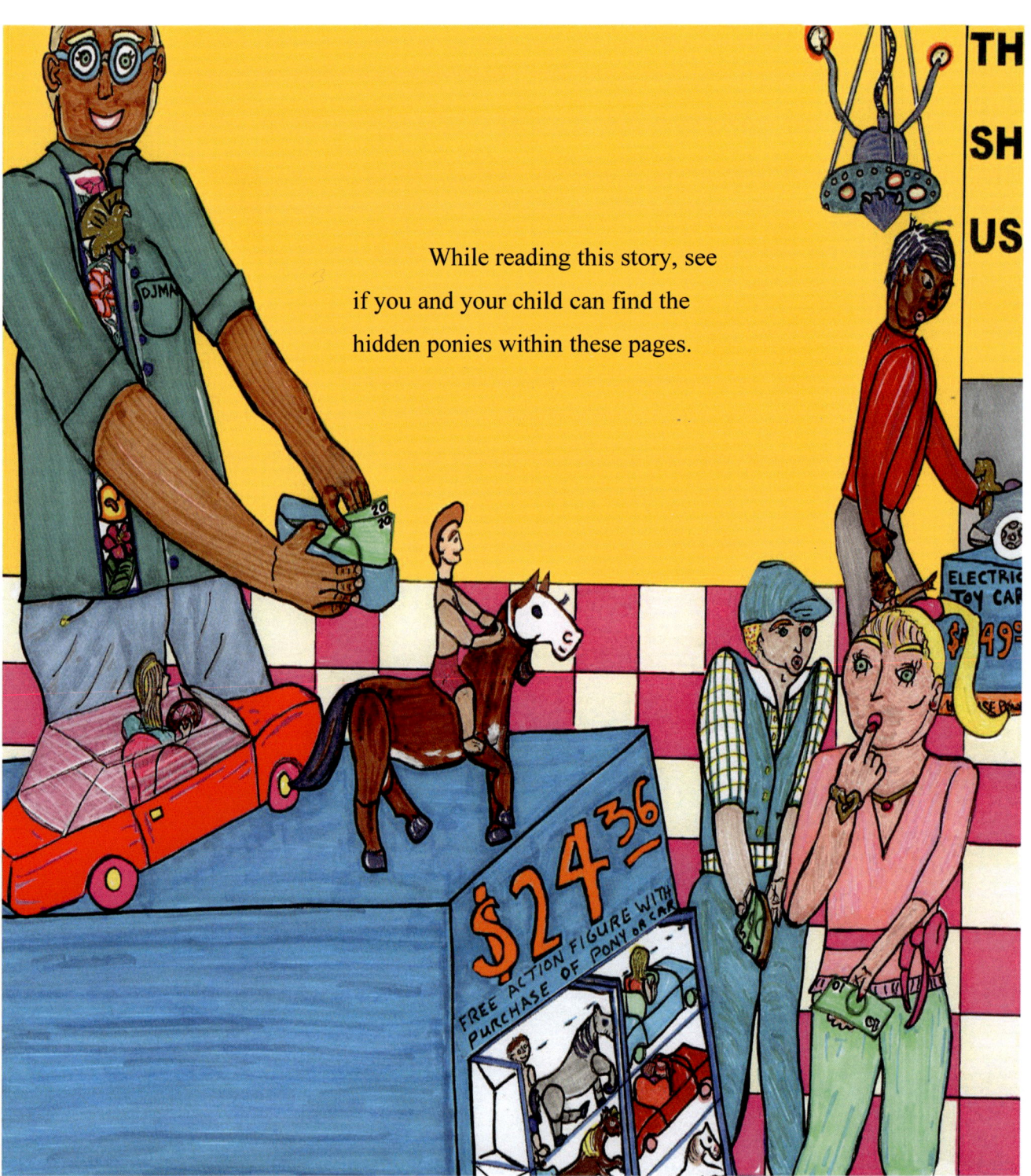

While reading this story, see if you and your child can find the hidden ponies within these pages.

The money has been cartoonized for legal reasons. Please display the real money to your child, pointing out the security measures embedded within it. Enjoy!

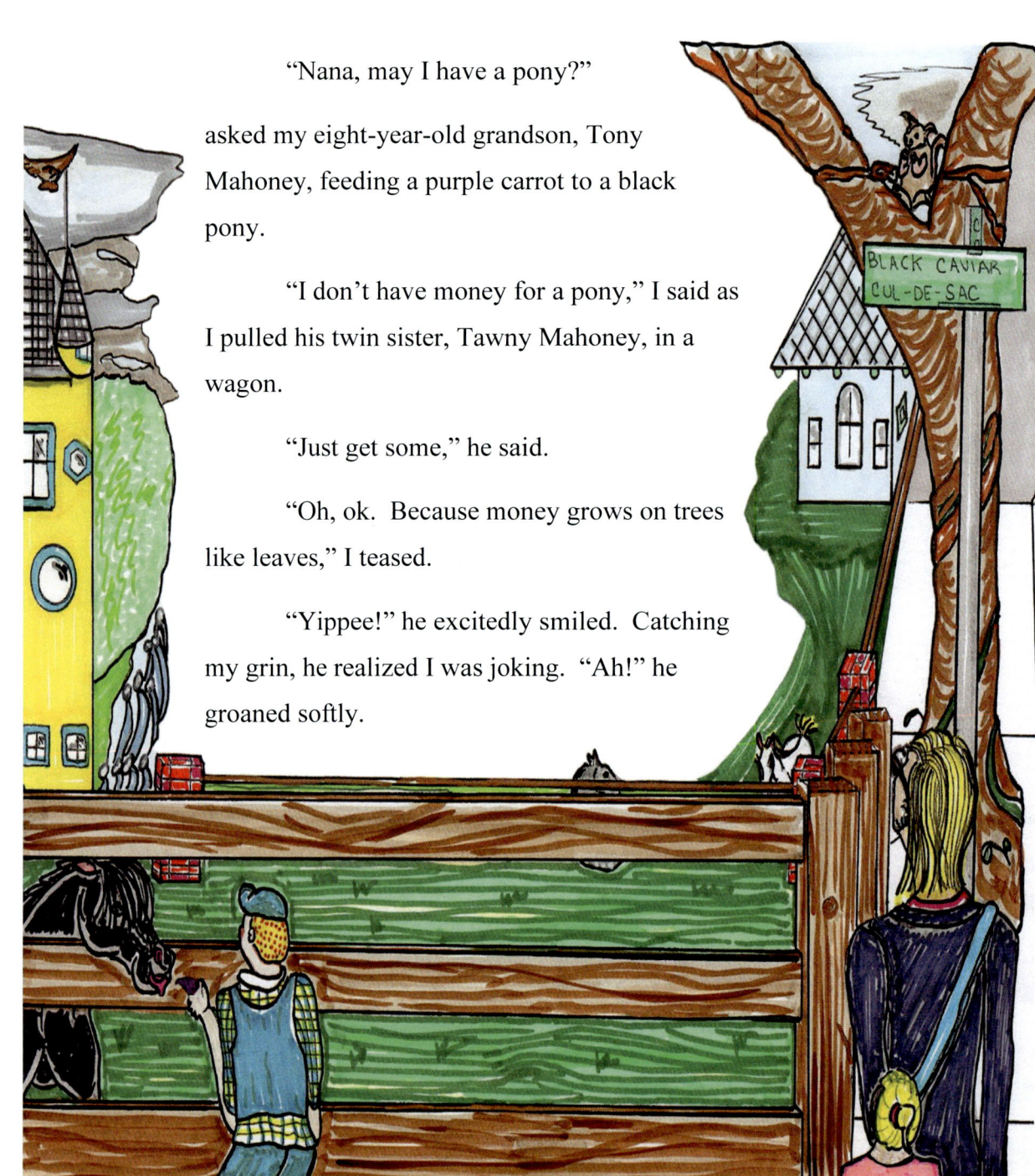

"Nana, may I have a pony?"

asked my eight-year-old grandson, Tony Mahoney, feeding a purple carrot to a black pony.

"I don't have money for a pony," I said as I pulled his twin sister, Tawny Mahoney, in a wagon.

"Just get some," he said.

"Oh, ok. Because money grows on trees like leaves," I teased.

"Yippee!" he excitedly smiled. Catching my grin, he realized I was joking. "Ah!" he groaned softly.

"How do I get money for a pony? Will you get me a job at your café? I can clean tables," he said.

"You are too young. Your work is to finish school." Glancing ahead on our path I said, pointing, "Look! Up ahead on the sidewalk!"

He closely followed my finger. His face lit up. "Money!" Surprised, he snatched it from the warm white sidewalk. Holding it up, he asked, "Will this buy me a noble steed?"

"Steed! My! What a grown-up word for such a little guy," I said, pausing. Putting on my glasses, I studied the shiny metal in his hand.

"It's orange with a man's face on it and a building on the other side," he said. He flipped it onto my palm for me to see it better.

"You have a penny. And it's copper, a sort of orange color," I said.

"Whose face is this?" Tony asked, pointing.

"That's President Lincoln. He freed the slaves," I said, handing it back to him.

Tony frowned, thinking out loud, "I thought there was a different president?"

"He lived a very long time ago. His face is on the penny so we don't forget what he did for us. That is his memorial building on the reverse side."

I began to tow Tawny down the street again in her wagon.

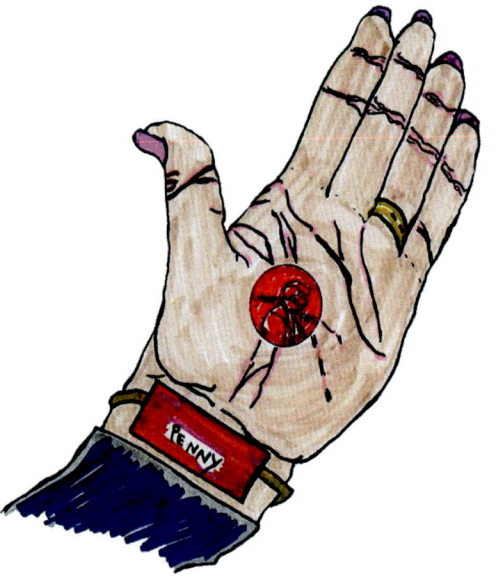

"Let me see!" Tawny demanded, holding her hand out. Gently Tony laid it in her palm. "It's pretty. I know those numbers. Two, zero, zero, five," she read.

Tony peeked over her shoulder, asking, "What's that?"

"That's the year it was minted," I said. We walked past a miniature horse gazing curiously at us.

"What's *minted*?" Tawny asked, slipping the penny into her pocket.

"The year it was made," I said.

"Hey! That's my penny! Go get your own," Tony shouted angrily, wrestling Tawny for it.

"I want a penny too for my pony!" Tawny whined, giving back the small coin.

"We will get you one, too," I promised.

"How many pennies do I need to get a pony?" Tony asked.

"I don't know how many pennies you will need to buy your pony. But a penny is one cent. There are one hundred pennies in a dollar," I said.

Bending over, he looked closely at the dark and rough driveway.

Seeing him, Tawny yelled, "Oh! That's my penny!" Quickly she jumped out of her purple and pink wagon. "Mine!"

The twins studied the round silver thing. "It's nothing," Tawny said, kicking it.

"No! It's minted." Tony saw the year 2014. He pinched the rolling, warm coin between his thumb and pointer finger. Holding it up, he showed them. "It's larger and grey."

"It's a nickel. And before you ask, it's five cents or five pennies." We continued our walk to the corner store. "You will need twenty nickels to make a dollar," I added.

"This doesn't look like President Lincoln," Tony said.

"You're correct. It's President Jefferson. He wrote the Declaration of Independence and fought for religious freedom and that's his home on the other side," I said.

Jumping on Tony, Tawny tried to wrestle it away from him, demanding, "Give it!"

"No! You didn't want it," Tony screamed.

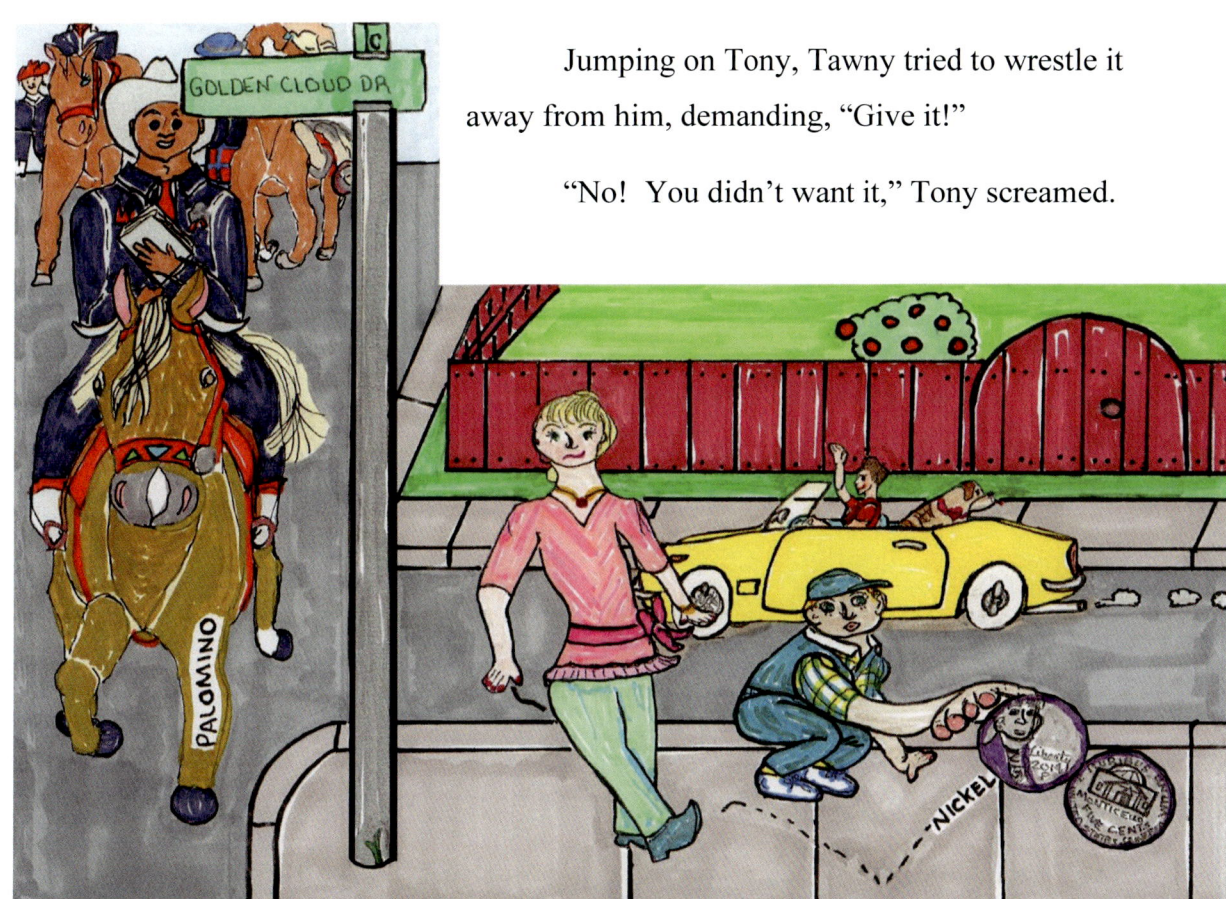

"Look! More pony money," I said, pointing to it. "What do you think it is?"

Tawny's clasp on the nickel loosened. "It's small. The smallest coin yet."

Tony yanked the nickel away. "It's all yours," he taunted, clanging his two coins together. "Two is more than one."

Holding up the small round silver coin, Tawny asked, "What is it, Nana?"

"You've got a dime," I said.

"And mine's bigger," Tony haughtily whispered in Tawny's ear, dashing away.

Tawny's lower lip stuck out as she was about to start crying. Bending down, I quietly said, "His is bigger but it's not the size that matters."

She brightened, turning her smile on me. "What do I got?"

"What do you have?" I corrected. "You have ten cents. Which is more than Tony's two coins put together."

Tawny leaned to the side and stared up at me, saying, "And I will need …?"

"Ten dimes make a dollar," I said.

Tony looked at his two coins, confused, "But two is more than one."

"True. You have more, but your coins don't equal what the dime equals," I said.

"So, who is this?" Tawny asked, rubbing his face clean with her thumb.

"President Franklin Roosevelt helped the poor, providing jobs and health care," I said.

"Why is there a fire torch on the back side?" Tawny asked.

"It's for liberty, the oak is for victory, and the olive is for peace," I said.

"What's more than a dime?" Tawny asked, skipping next to the wagon.

"There are a lot that are worth more than a dime. There's the quarter. It's worth twenty-five cents. Four quarters make up a dollar," I said, pulling out a quarter from my pocket.

"What great man's face is on that one?" Tony asked, taking it in his hand to get a closer look. Tawny closely studied the warm silver coin he held in his hand. Then he returned it to me.

"George Washington," I said, arriving at the store. I left the wagon near the front door.

Tawny wanted to know, "Did he free the slaves too?"

Tony pulled on the heavy front door, slowly opening it.

"Thank you, young man." Happily I praised him as I entered the shop. "No, he was the first President of America, the Father of this country. He fought for freedom from a mean king."

Tawny frowned, complaining, "How come there aren't any women on any coins?"

"Oh, but there are!" I said, walking down the cookie aisle. "There's the Lady Liberty, the Susan B. Anthony, and the Sacagawea coin." I grabbed a gallon of milk from the fridge.

"The what?" Tony interrupted.

"Sacagawea and Susan B. Anthony are large coins, and they equal a dollar. Susan B. Anthony has her face on the head side of the coin. The reverse side has a faraway earth, stars and a stretched-out eagle landing on the moon," I said, heading back to the front.

"Oh! I want that one," Tawny said.

"Very few people get rid of their Susan B. Anthony coins. And there was only a small amount minted." I laid the milk on the counter in front of Kent, the clerk.

Picking up a pack of gum, Tony asked, "What about Saca something?" He held the gum up to me pleadingly.

Softly I said to him, "You have to choose. Money for a pony or gum. Which one do you want?" Making a face, he put it back. I continued, "Sacagawea is an American Indian woman who helped Lewis and Clark map out America when it was still wild and untamed.

Giggling, Tony said, "Clark sounds like clerk."

"Yes it does." Kent smiled. He scanned the white milk with a red light, saying, "That will be $4.29 (four dollars and twenty-nine cents). I have a Sacagawea coin. Do you want to see it?"

"Yes! Yes! Yes!" They shouted happily, jumping up and down.

He hit a button on his silver cash register. The brown money drawer popped open.

Dragging a large gold coin out, he held it up. "The Sacagawea

coin, obverse side."

"What's that?" Tawny whispered to Tony.

Hearing her, Kent said, "The side with the head on it."

Leaning closer, they squinted carefully at it. "Hey!

There's a baby on her back!" Tawny said, impressed.

"Her son. An eagle is on the reverse," Kent said.

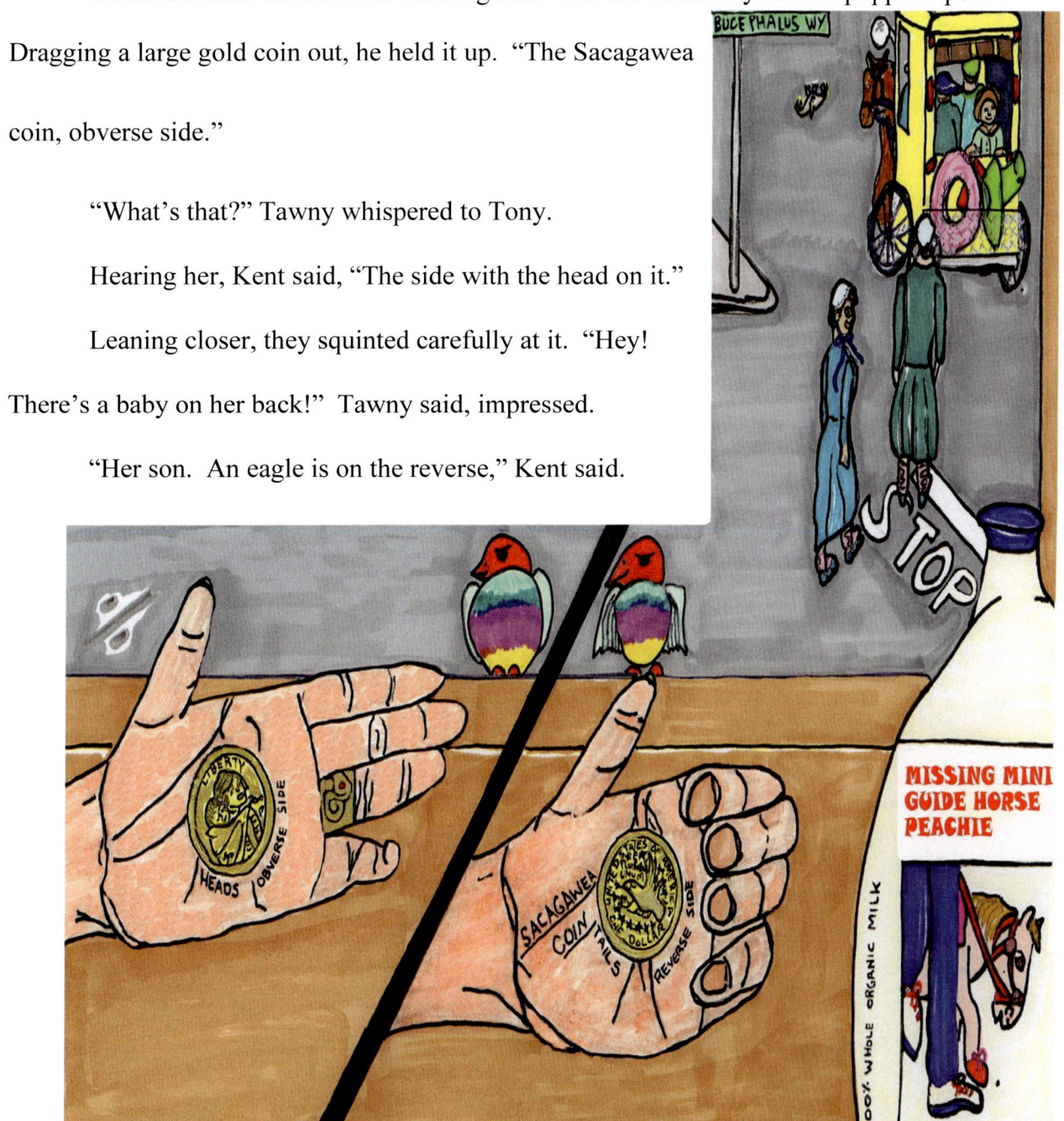

In my blue wallet, I fished around for four one-dollar bills. Tawny pulled them out of my hand. Shuffling through them, she studied the face on each. "That's George Washington! I remember because he's on the quarter."

"Yep." I let her study the money, presenting a five-dollar bill to Kent instead. But Tawny quickly snatched that too.

"They are both green," she saw.

"All United States of America paper money is green," Kent said. "That's why it's also affectionately called Lettuce, Kale, or Greenbacks."

"Or Bread," Tony added. "Bucks, Chips, Dough."

"Dead Presidents," I mumbled, gently taking the five from Tawny.

"President Lincoln," Tawny shouted, pointing to it.

"Very good!" Kent approved, taking it. Counting out my change, he palmed two quarters, two dimes, and a shiny copper penny, handing me seventy-one cents ($0.71).

"And who is this?" Kent held up a ten.

A businessman slid up behind us. "Um… a dead President?" Tony guessed.

"Hamilton. Not a dead President," the businessman answered.

"Then who is he?" Tawny asked, looking up at the stranger.

"A man who founded the current banking system." Flicking the reverse side of the ten-dollar bill Kent still held up, he added, "See? The Treasury Department. Would you ring me up please?" He lifted up his black coffee and orange Cheetos for the clerk to see.

"The White House looks like the Treasury Department," Tawny said.

Smiling, I applauded.

"Very good."

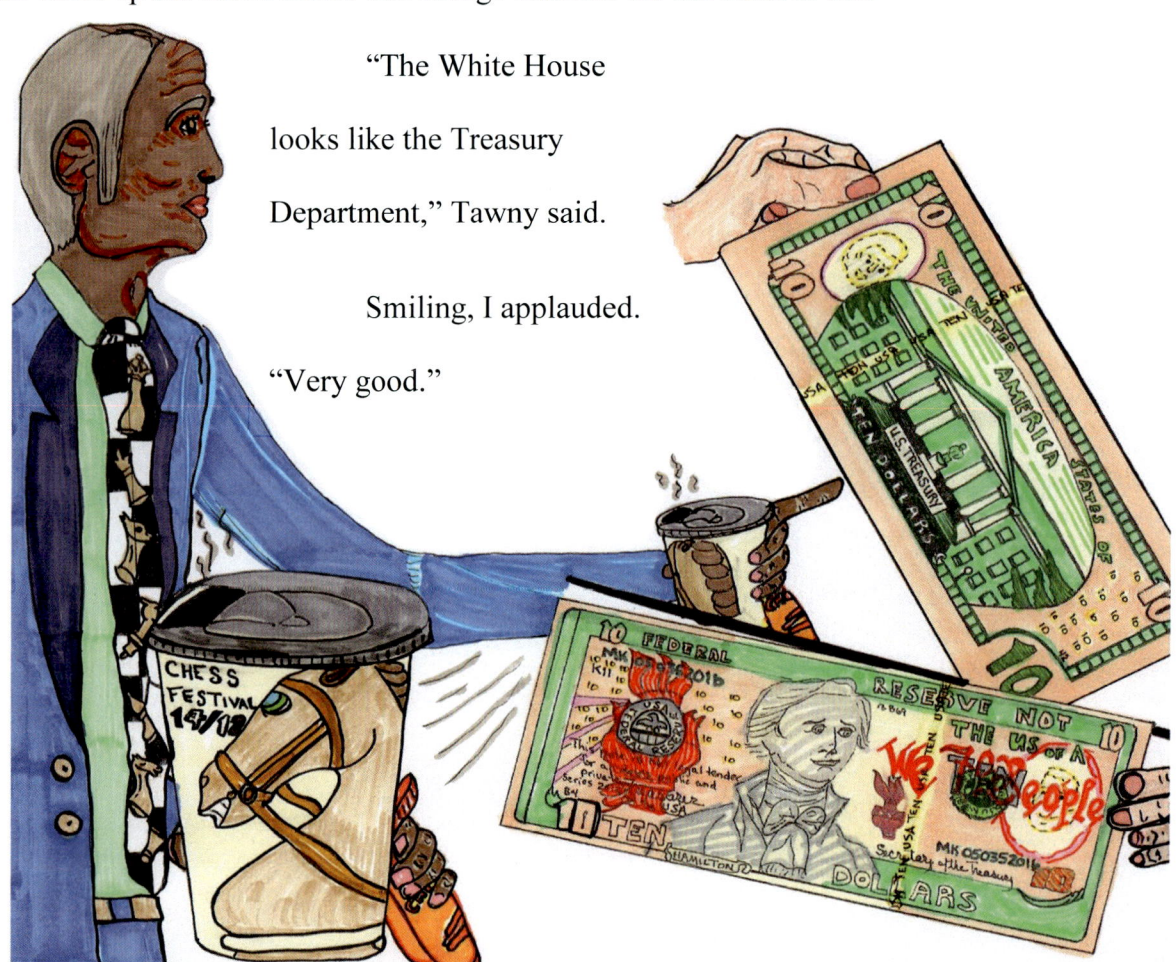

Having rung him up, Kent said, "Four dollars ($4.00), please."

The businessman pulled out a twenty from his red leather wallet. "This is a dead President. President Andrew Jackson. But I think he doesn't belong on it." He allowed Tony and Tawny to glance at it briefly before handing it over.

"Hmph!" Kent huffed. "Your change, sir, sixteen dollars ($16.00)." He counted out a ten, a five, and a one-dollar bill.

"Why not?" Tony demanded.

Taking the bills, he told Tony, "He was against banks. Bye." He left.

"What's the biggest buck you've ever gotten?" Tony asked, looking questioningly up at the store owner.

Leaning against the counter, Kent answered, "Mm…I've gotten plenty of fifties and hundreds."

"Are they dead Presidents too?" Tawny asked, hopping up and down on one foot.

"One is. President Ulysses S. Grant, who fought under President Lincoln to keep America united during the Civil War and free the slaves. And the reverse side," he said, slapping a fifty on the counter. The twins crowded around to study the large bill with the United States Capitol on the backside.

"And the other one," he said, replacing the fifty-dollar bill with a hundred-dollar bill, "is a great inventor."

"What did the great inventor make?" Tawny asked. Grabbing the counter top, she rose on tippy-toe to stare hard at the bill.

"Benjamin Franklin wrote the Bill of Independence, which is why the Independence Hall is on the reverse side. He talked the French into helping America with the money needed to win freedom from a harsh king. He invented the stove, bifocal glasses like your Nana wears, and then there is his work with electricity."

"Wow!" Tawny said.

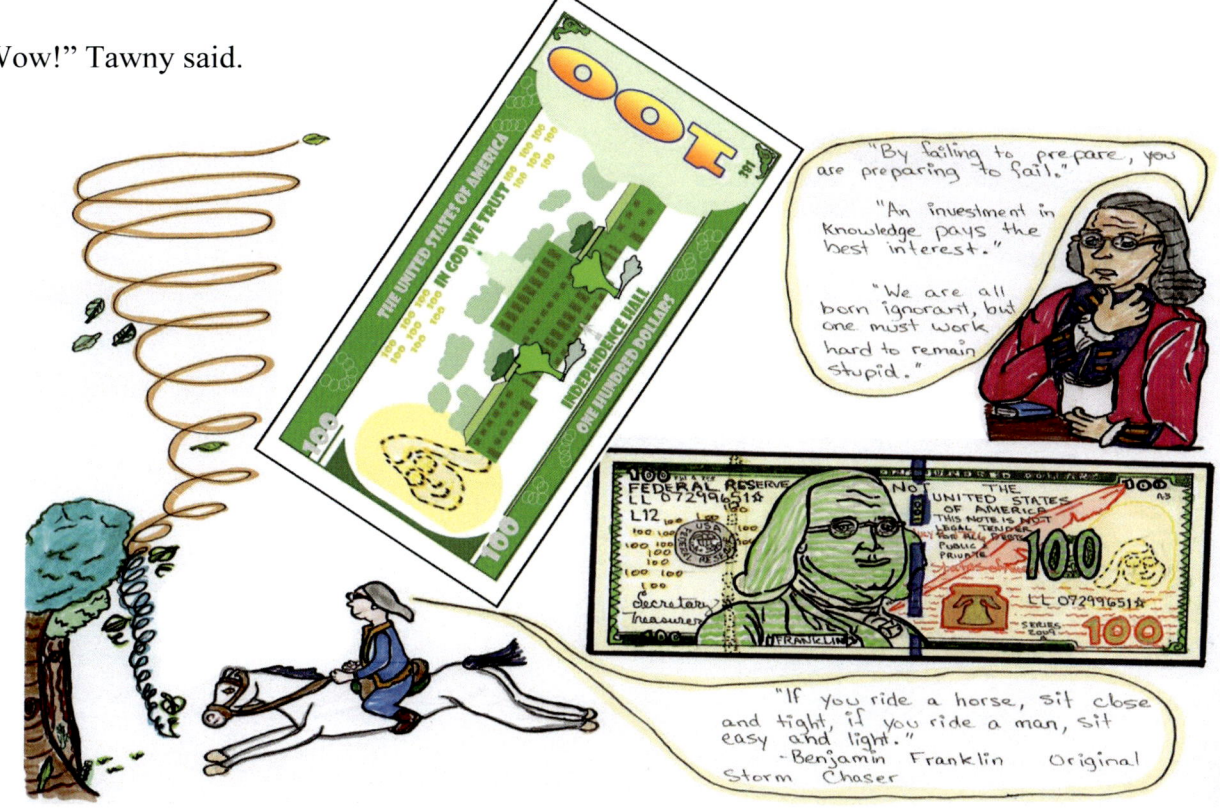

Kent shoved the money away. "And this is the most expensive coin with a lady on it." Kent presented a shiny new gold coin with an African American Lady Liberty minted in 2017 for our inspection. "It has a face value of one hundred dollars but it's so rare we sell it for $342.93 (three hundred forty-two dollars and ninety-three cents). That's called a Numismatic coin."

`   "Ahh!" Tawny exclaimed. In awe, she rubbed the beautiful coin. "She's pretty."

Outside, I suggested, "Let's go to rancher Chander's farm. He'll let us ride one of his ponies."

"I want to ride the golden palomino," Tawny said, running ahead.

"You can have her. I want the buckskin. Race you there!" Tony said. Dashing by, he playfully slapped her ponytail in her face. "Last one there is a rotten egg!"

"Don't get too far ahead!" I called after them.

"Well, hello!" Young Chander greeted us. "What can I do for you today?" The tall, thin rancher said, dropping hay in front of a beautiful dappled, curly haired donkey baby.

"We want to ride one of your ponies, please," they said together, eagerly bouncing up and down.

Pointing to the golden horse with the white mane and tail, Tawny sang, "I want to ride your palomino."

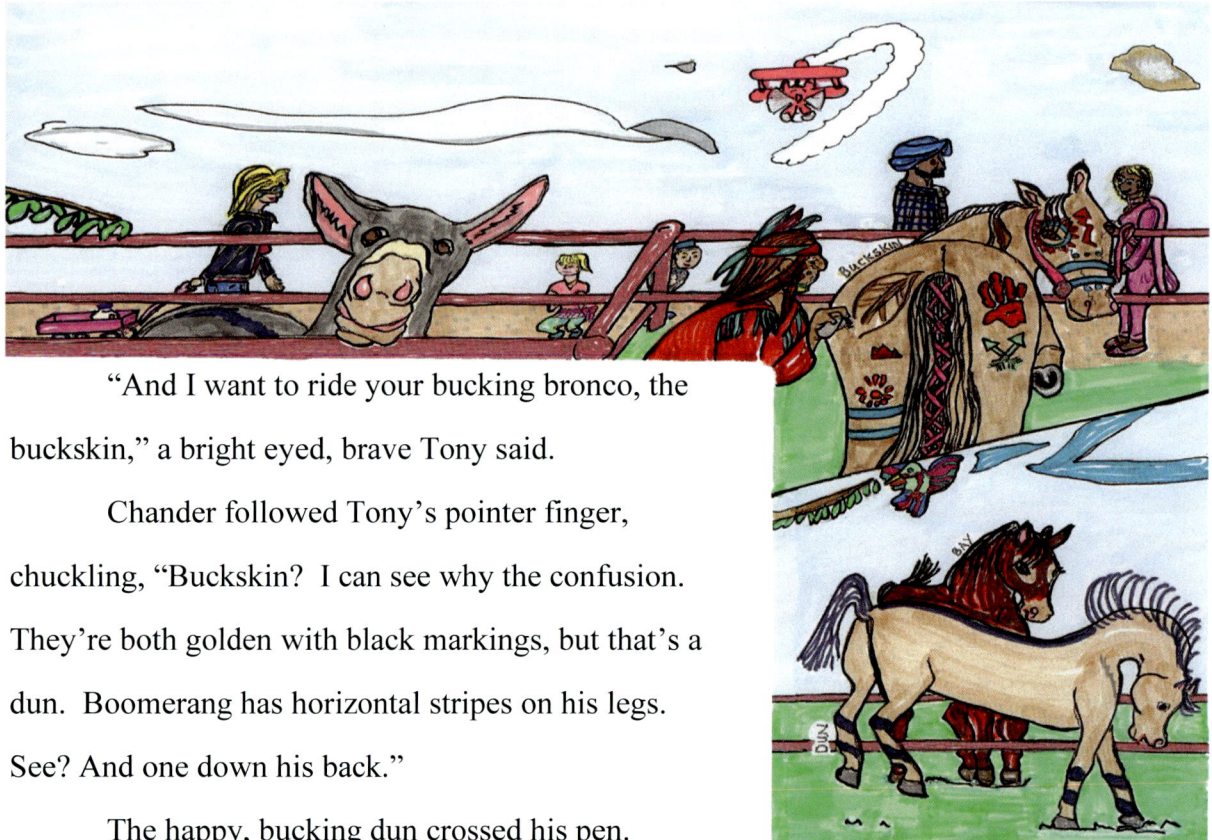

"And I want to ride your bucking bronco, the buckskin," a bright eyed, brave Tony said.

Chander followed Tony's pointer finger, chuckling, "Buckskin? I can see why the confusion. They're both golden with black markings, but that's a dun. Boomerang has horizontal stripes on his legs. See? And one down his back."

The happy, bucking dun crossed his pen.

"Sadly, he's not saddle broke yet," Chander told him. "But I could put you on good ol' Jingles. She's a little darker, a bay pony. What do you think?" He nodded towards the gentle mare or female pony.

Tony, unsure, frowned, mumbling, "She looks asleep."

"She'll perk right up when you get on her," Chander promised.

"You can't!" Sania, a blond woman insisted from the barn, walking towards us. Joining the group, she stopped. "Ol' Jingles has tendonitis or a swollen foot. She's not going anywhere."

"Sorry to hear that." I frowned. Glancing about, I came across a gorgeous pony. "What about that strawberry roan there?" I said to Tony.

Chander looked up. "Rohita's a bit sluggish but she'll do," he told Tony.

"I don't see any strawberries," Tawny complained.

We laughed. "That's the name of her color," I said.

Tawny, confused, looked once more. "But she's not red. She's …mostly white."

"And that's why she's called a roan," Chander huffed, lifting a saddle onto Rohita's back.

"Here, I'll put your milk in the fridge," Sania offered, leaving with our milk.

Hunched over, Chander twisted at the waist to look at me, saying, "So Mrs. K, what will it be?" He tightened the cinch or belt around the roan's girth or belly.

Slowly I looked around his group of ponies. "Hmm, how about that Appaloosa?"

"Which one?" Chander asked. Straightening up, Chander dropped the stirrup gently against the roan's side. "The Snow Flake Blanket or the Leopard Appaloosa?"

"Snow Flake Blanket?" Tawny kicked up her foot and caught her ankle behind her back. Dancing a jig on one leg, she said, "That's a cute name for a horse."

"It's a kind of polka-dotted horse. Doesn't it look like it got caught in a snow storm and was covered with snow flakes?" Chander asked.

Planting her leg, Tawny curiously looked over the railing at the mare or mommy horse. "Yeah. But where's the palomino?" Chander waved them over to the palomino male or stallion.

He patted the palomino's saddle. "Up you go." Grinning largely, Tawny allowed Chander to lift her up onto the pink saddle, between the cantle and horn.

"Keep your hands on the horn and reins," Chander said. "Head up, back straight, heels down."

She did. "There you go!" we said proudly, smiling on her.

Gold Nugget turned his head to stare curiously at Tawny. "He's sizing you up or judging you," I told her. "Kindly let him know who's the boss."

"I will," she confidently said.

"Well, young man?" Chander asked, hands on hips.

Tony pointed. "That one!"

Curiously we looked over Gold Nugget's shoulders. A paint chewing on oats stared unblinking back at us. Tony cried, "The Mustang! An American Indian horse."

"I don't know. Red's mighty feisty. I think he's too much horse for you," Chander said. Grinning, he winked at me, jokingly.

Tony nodded decisively. "He's the one for me. Nana, you can have Rohita."

Atop the paint, Tony impatiently urged Red into a gallop. The palomino, Gold Nugget, who was not wishing to be left behind, broke out into a canter. Neck and neck, they raced around the arena, turning up the dirt. "Yee-Ha!" The twins shouted happily, passing me. Good-naturedly, Rohita the roan and I followed at a nice, steady pace.

"I won! I won! I won!" Tony shouted, hands overhead.

"You did not!" Tawny cried. "I did. Me and Gold Nugget."

Chander smiled, grabbing their reins. "I'd say you both won."

"There can be only one winner," Tony said.

"Neither one of you paid for your rides and you very much enjoyed yourselves. So I'd say there is more than one winner here today." Gently Chander lifted the twins off their saddle and set them on their feet.

"Do you know where I can get some money to buy Gold Nugget?" Tawny asked, petting his silky mane.

"Gold Nugget isn't for sale. He's too valuable to us. But maybe we could work out a deal," Chander's eyebrows rose, thinking about it out loud.

Tawny clapped joyfully. "Yes!"

"Hey! I want in on this deal," Tony jealously whined.

"From time to time, we need someone to muck out, or clean up the horse's stalls. It won't be too hard. Maybe you could clean them out for a free pony ride and twenty dollars a month?" Chander offered.

Tawny nodded. "How long would that take?"

"It would just be one or two hours, every other weekend. It would allow you plenty of time for school, for riding, and your family." Chander dropped Tawny's hand and stood up. "Maybe you could start right now?" Catching Tony's jealous eye, he added, "Both of you?"

"Yes!" Tony shouted with a smile, holding his hand out. Grinning, Chander briefly took it.

"This way," Chander said. They nodded, following him into the stables.

Quickly they mucked out the stalls. The ponies were sweet and friendly, letting them do their duty, while a twitchy cat sat down to watch them.

Back at our house, I happily began to browse the internet with them for pony ads. "This horse's name is Sparkles and she's only $300.00 (three hundred dollars)," I read.

"And she's beautiful! Like her name. Three hundred dollars won't take me long to save up for her," Tawny said.

I continued reading Sparkles good qualities on HorseTrader.com. I frowned, reading about the Cremello's or white pony's good points. "It says here, she's not broke."

"I'm glad she's not broken," Tawny said, handing me my cell phone. "This is my next pony."

I refused to take the phone. Putting an arm around her shoulders, I gently said, "Baby girl, broke means she's not educated yet in riding and saddlery. She'll hurt you if you try to ride her."

Saddened, she let the phone go, watching it skid across the oak dining room table. "I'm never going to get a pony," she whined.

"Yes, you will." Tapping on the Free Rescue Horses tab, we glanced at the list of horses rescued and needing a new home. "Look! You may adopt this palomino for $450 (four hundred fifty dollars). You'll be able to afford that soon enough. And she's ride-able," I told her.

Tawny smiled and reached for the phone once more. "Let's call."

Tony interrupted, "They don't have any paints." He sat back on his knees, frowning at the tablet.

"It's ok if you don't find what you want right away. It'll come to you. Just continue looking," I encouraged him, rubbing his back.

"I know what I want," he said, pointing out the large window to across the street. We looked curiously at the neighbor's empty pen. It was blocked by an excited, happy family passing by on their ponies. "That one!"

"Which one?" Tawny asked.

"The black one? The appaloosa? Or the buckskin?" I asked, studying the ponies clattering noisily across the street.

"No, no, no. Not those. A Mustang," he said. "A red one."

"There are no red Mustangs," I said, looking again.

"Va-room, va-room-room!" roared a sporty vehicle. It came within view from behind the neighbor's flowering plants. It stopped, allowing the ponies to gallop by.

"Oh!" I said. "A red Mustang!"

"Papa! Papa John's home," the twins cried. "With Shelby."

Outside, we crowded around the hot pink Shelby Mustang car and Papa John. Happily the twins hugged him, one on each side. With an arm about both of them, he joyfully asked, "So have you been good for Nana?"

"Of course! Always!" they promised.

"We've got pony money." Tawny held up her handful of money. She continued, "I'm going to get a palomino."

"Where'd you get all that money?" he said, amazed.

"We found it," Tony pointed towards his chest and said, "I'm going to get a red Mustang."

His eyebrows rose at that. "Oh, really?!"
Papa John said, surprised.

"Like Shelby," Tony bragged.

"Ok. We can work on it together when you
do," Papa John offered, ruffling Tony's hair.

Tony smiled. Turning, he ran inside. "I'm going
to look for one right now."

"Me too. But I want a palomino mare," Tawny said, running after him.

I smiled at Papa John. "Missed you, Baby!"

He laughed, "Are you sure you mean me? Or Shelby?"

"You! You big lug," I teased, leaning in to kiss him.

Tossing an arm around my waist, he said, "Shelby's as good as new now." With his other hand, he held up my keys.

Eagerly I took them. And as we walked up the drive, I looked back to whisper to Shelby, "Missed you, Baby!"

Softly Papa John laughed.

"Whose turn is it to count my change?" I asked, a few years later, pulling out coins from my black pants.

"Me! Me! I get to keep the change from your waitressing tips if I can count it." An eager twelve-year-old Tawny reminded me, holding out her cupped hands. Gently I gave them to her.

Papa John brought over his specially marked cup that counts change, called a change cup and Tony brought the paper coin rolls. These are special tubes that you fill with only one kind of coin. When full, you pinch the ends shut. The rolls tell you how much coins are in a roll. Tawny counted the change. Papa John poured the nickels into the change cup and Tony rolled them up.

"I have $2.53 (two dollars and fifty-three cents)," Tawny said proudly. "That brings my balance up to $2,609.55 (two thousand six hundred nine dollars and fifty-five cents)."

"And I have $2,614.01 (two thousand six hundred fourteen dollars and one cent). I found some cans at school that I cashed in. May we go look at that pony car we saw today? I only need $35.99 (thirty-five dollars and ninety-nine cents) and then I can buy it. Maybe the owner will hold it for me," Tony said, hopeful.

"When you buy a pony or a car, never pay full price. We will offer them a deal they cannot refuse $2,500 (two thousand five hundred dollars). That's called, 'negotiations'," Papa

John said, getting up. "Let's go!"

"Nana, come look at what we got!" Tony said proudly, bursting through the kitchen door later on that day. Inside the garage, I looked at the dirty Mustang. "I don't remember the number of ponies or horses it has under the hood but it's a lot."

"Horses? What horses are under the hood?" Tawny asked. We smiled.

"The power a horse has in pulling. Anything with an engine is said to have the same power as a horse (hp). This engine has 200hp but it will have 350 hp when we are done," Papa John answered.

"Papa John calls it promising." Pointing to the large scratch, he added, "We can fix this and paint it black

and red. Check it out!"

He held up a rough drawing of what he wanted the pony car to look like and I knew I was looking at his future car.

THE END!

Or is it?

Did you find the hidden ponies in their pens? Pastures? Did you find them hidden in rings and bracelets? Purses, wallets? Ties? On toys? Cups? On cars and trucks? There are over 50 (fifty) hidden ponies.

Perhaps you were paying attention to the street signs? Black Caviar Cul-de-sac, Golden Cloud Drive, Bucephalus Way, and Chetak Street? These streets are all named after famous horses and ponies. Do you know them? How did they contribute to our history? May you and your family have fun finding out.

Thank you!